TREASURES FROM THE SANCTUARY

FOR THE

———————— ✿ ————————

MIND

TREASURES FROM THE SANCTUARY

FOR THE

MIND

Tanya Wheway

with Jane Ross-Macdonald

Thorsons
An Imprint of HarperCollins*Publishers*

Thorsons
An Imprint of HarperCollins*Publishers*
77–85 Fulham Palace Road
Hammersmith, London W6 8JB

Published by Thorsons 1998
1 3 5 7 9 10 8 6 4 2

A catalogue record for this book
is available from the British Library

ISBN 0 7225 3769 7

The quotes given in this series of books for the
Mind, Body and Spirit form part of a collection
Tanya Wheway has gathered over many years. For this
reason not all of them are attributed, but the publishers
are anxious to trace any copyright holders that have
not been contacted for permission.

The Sanctuary and the Single Fish Device are the trade mark
of The Sanctuary at Covent Garden Ltd

Text illustrations by Daisy Kelly

Printed and bound in Great Britain by
Woolnoughs Bookbinding Ltd, Irthlingborough, Northants

DEDICATION

I would like to dedicate this set of three books for the mind, body and spirit to my amazingly wonderful family who I love very dearly: husband, business partner and lover, Allan, son Mark and his wife Katherine, daughter Samantha, her husband Jon and grandchildren Emily-Anne and James, also my great parents, Micky and Norman. They have all really made my life totally complete and I would like to thank them for all their love, and also for their understanding and the support they have always given me in respect of all the hours I spend working.

I would like to thank the Sanctuary team for their assistance and support. A very big thank you to Jane Ross-Macdonald for all that she has contributed to the book and for keeping me on track, to Wanda Whitely for opening the doors and being such an inspiration and Nicola Vimpany for her tremendous patience and warm, experienced support.

PREFACE

The Sanctuary in Covent Garden, London, came of age in 1998 as it celebrated its 21st anniversary as a Day Spa exclusively for women. In celebration we have launched this series of *Treasures from the Sanctuary:* one for the *Mind,* one for the *Body* and one for the *Spirit.* We hope they will provide you with words of wisdom and wit to inform, amuse and inspire.

In 1964 an American dancer/choreographer, Gary Cockrell, opened our London premises as the famous Dance Centre, frequented by talented dancers and actors such as Nureyev, Gene Kelly, Dustin Hoffman and Sir John Gielgud. Today the tradition of exercising the body continues with The Sanctuary Fitness Club, exclusively for women.

The Sanctuary philosophy is a holistic one, encompassing mind, body and spirit, which nurtures all the senses. Paintings and candlelight delight the eye, essential oils fragrance the air, fresh produce titillates the taste buds, expert hands pamper the body and the sound of fountains and beautiful music soothe the mind and soul.

INTRODUCTION

'The mind is like a flower – very beautiful when it is open.'

I have been immersed in the 'people business' for over 30 years, working in the fields of positive health, nutrition, fitness, beauty, stress management, personal development and complementary medicine. I firmly believe that *the mind is where it is at*. If you get the way you think right then so many things automatically fall into place; likewise if the way you think is not in good shape then it is likely that your life, work, relationships and health will also be in poor shape.

The mind is the key to so very much, and we have only just begun to scratch the surface of its capabilities. Learn to unleash its power, but direct it well. It is important that we do not allow our minds to become blinkered, that we nurture our inquisitive nature and that we use our minds to make good things happen for ourselves, our family, our friends and our world.

We hope that this little book will give you positive assistance and support on your personal journey.

Warmest wishes from the Sanctuary team.

Tanya Wheway
Managing Director
The Sanctuary, Covent Garden

HOW TO USE THIS BOOK

We need to open our minds and think creatively and positively if we are to maximize the opportunities and overcome the challenges that surround us.

The power of the mind is truly phenomenal. It has the power to be destructive or to achieve positive results in all aspects of our lives. Having your mind work for you, instead of against you, can bring you the two most treasured possessions: health and happiness. If you have these, what more do you need or want?

Respecting that everyone's time is incredibly precious, and usually in short supply, we have created a style that is easy to dip into. The alphabetical listing will enable you to find material that is appropriate for you.

The quotes given in our series of books for the mind, body and spirit form part of a collection I have made over many years. I hope you find them useful, inspirational and amusing.

'Instead of pouring knowledge into people's heads,
we need to help them grind a new set of eyeglasses
so that we can see the world in a new way.

J. S. Brown

ACTION

'The surest way to go broke is to sit around waiting for a break.'

'A journey of a thousand miles begins with a single step.'
Chairman Mao

'Two of the saddest words in the English language are: too late.'

It is all too easy to get stuck in a rut. The same old job, the same old relationship, the same old bad habits. Recognizing our 'stuckness' is the first task – and you may be startled at how long you have allowed an unhealthy situation to continue. Making a decision to make a positive change is the next step. We all fear change, we all fear self-exposure and we all fear failure – but remember, in doing nothing you are also making a choice. Take control of your own future. Go for the life you really want.

'Whether you think you can, or whether you think you can't, you're right.'

Mary Kay Ash

'What you say, so shall you think, so shall you do, so shall you be.'

'I am a serene, free, valuable woman, trusting myself to risk, unconditionally loving myself and others.'

Affirmation of a Champneys' guest

AFFIRMATIONS

Over the years I have often heard people saying, as they left our health resorts, that they were going to try to take more exercise, lose weight or relax more. As soon as I hear the word 'try' I know they are likely to fail.

Affirmations are simply positive statements that you repeat to yourself. They work because we tend to believe what we tell ourselves, especially if we say it over and over again. Affirmations are one way we can programme ourselves for success, and to work they must start with 'I', be in the present tense and not contain any negative words.

It won't happen instantly – remember you do have to work at these. The best times are first thing in the morning and last thing at night. They take time, effort and repetition. And as you progress, celebrate what you have achieved; don't dwell on what you still have yet to do.

*'Anger is a signal, and one worth listening to.
Our anger may be a message that we are being hurt,
that our rights are being violated, that our needs or
wants are not being adequately met, or simply that
something may not be right.'*

Harriet Goldhor Lerner

'To jaw-jaw is always better than to war-war.'

Winston Churchill

*'For every minute you are angry you lose sixty
seconds of happiness.'*

Ralph Waldo Emerson

*'People who fight fire with fire usually end up with
ashes.'*

Abigail VanBuren

ANGER

I believe God gave us many different feelings and there is nothing wrong with any of them in the right place at the right time. Sometimes we need to get angry to right wrongs and make things happen. But the danger comes when you hold on to these sort of feelings for too long. Then they become destructive, like a burning piece of coal that you are holding in your hand – and the person it's burning is you. It is important to use it to achieve something, and then let it go.

Tips for anger management:

1 Take a few deep breaths and try to assess the situation objectively.
2 Remind yourself that no one is perfect, including yourself.
3 Do something physical: bash a pillow in private, go for a walk or a work out.
4 Put your thoughts on paper: this can help put things in perspective and exorcise some of your anger.
5 Work out the most effective way of dealing with the situation, looking to achieve a really positive result, not just retribution.
6 Sometimes it helps to talk it through with a close family member or friend.
7 Don't 'bank-account' it, if you can't forget it, address the issues calmly and constructively with the person in question while it is still fresh in your mind and theirs.
8 Apologize if you could have handled things better: this often helps the other person to be more forthcoming in their apologies.

'I keep the telephone of my mind open to peace, harmony, health, love and abundance. Then whenever doubt, anxiety, or fear try to call me, they keep getting a busy signal and soon they'll forget my number.'

Edith Armstrong

ANXIETY

Long-term anxiety is psychologically draining and can make you more susceptible to illness. While counselling can help, so can the following:

1 Reduce consumption of caffeine, alcohol and recreational drugs.
2 Take a vitamin B6 supplement.
3 Have a massage with lavender, or swirl a few drops into your bath.
4 Valerian tea, ginseng and Rescue Remedy are recommended.
5 Learn relaxation techniques or go to a yoga class.
6 Learn deep breathing exercises (*see Treasures from the Sanctuary for the Body*).
7 Affirmations and visualization are techniques that can be very helpful (*see p3 and p128*).
8 Avoid drug therapy if you can. It does not impact on the cause of the problem and may have side-effects.

'You can get an enormous amount done with
some tact, some charm, a smile ... and persistence.'
Tanya Wheway

ASSERTIVENESS

Assertiveness does not mean aggressiveness. It means having belief in yourself, and respect for yourself and others. It means:

- being able to say 'no' without feeling guilty
- standing up for yourself, by using sentences that start with 'I'
- expressing anger constructively
- asking for what you want in a clear, specific and positive way
- putting yourself forward in a positive light
- listening to criticism without over-reacting, and assessing its truth or otherwise
- doing your homework so that you can speak authoritatively, with knowledge and, where appropriate, with a strong case to put forward.
- like a child, not accepting the first 'no' as final.

'Attitude is a little thing that makes a big difference.'

'Change your thinking and you change your life.'
Earl Nightingale

'The pleasure you get from your life is equal to the attitude you put into it.'

'It's a funny thing about life: if you refuse to accept anything but the best, you very often get it.'
W. Somerset Maugham

ATTITUDE

I'm sure we can all think of examples of men and women who have achieved unbelievable things, such as the man who walked 3,000 miles across America. What made this particularly remarkable was the fact that he did it on his hands because he had no legs. The difference between a winner and a loser is quite often the difference between those who have dreams and determination and those who don't. People who use excuses for not achieving are in danger of putting iron bars around their lives and living in a prison of their own making.

A positive attitude can achieve what might, at the time, seem like the impossible. Work at developing a very positive attitude within yourself, and also do what you can to encourage it in others, especially in all children whose lives you impact on so much. Conversely, refuse to allow cynical and negative thoughts to become part of your make-up and actions.

BAD HABITS

*'Check your motivation (who gains?), examine the
habit, set goals, practise, monitor progress, reward.'*
Gael Lindenfield

*'That was me. That was my nature. Just because
I have been that way in the past does not mean
I have to be that way in the future.'*
Dr Wayne Dyer

What are bad habits? Smoking, over-eating, busy-ness,
controlling behaviour, workaholism, perfectionism … the
list goes on. You will know what yours are and which ones
you would like to change. It is not easy to change habits,
but it is certainly achievable. One problem is that many of
us have programmed ourselves to believe that we cannot
change things; 'that's me' 'that's my nature'. Use an affirmation to start to visualize a different you.

Hypnotherapy, aversion therapy and acupuncture can also help, but practical steps you can take yourself are:

1 Examine your motivation: what do I gain from this habit? If your current actions and behaviour only produce negative results, surely it's worth the effort to change them?
2 What is the habit? How is it manifest?
3 Set measurable and realistic goals.
4 Persist!
5 Monitor your progress.
6 Give yourself rewards as milestones are reached.

BALANCE

'Balance is the key to success in all things.'
Tanya Wheway

Balance is a hard thing to achieve, but something always to strive for. You can exercise too little, but you can also exercise too much. You can care too little, or even too much. You can become a health fanatic – and that ain't healthy. Balance is the key to everything: the balance between work and play, the harmony within our bodies and between our mind, body and spirit – as well as the ecological balance of our planet. It is what the Buddhists call the 'middle road'. Once you step off this path you head into danger zones which may lead you towards mental or physical illness, idleness or fanaticism.

Does your life feel in balance? If not, this is something to address sooner rather than later. (*See Stress p3, Affirmations p122 and Visualization p128.*)

BILL OF RIGHTS

I have the right to be treated with respect.

I have the right not to take responsibility for anyone
    else's problems or bad behaviour.

I have the right to get angry.

I have the right to say NO.

I have the right to make mistakes and ask for help.

I have the right to have my own feelings and opinions.

I have the right to negotiate for change.

I have the right to change my mind.

I have the right to protest unfair treatment.

Every right has a corresponding obligation.

'Beware of those who always like to blame, for they shall inherit very little that is good.'

Tanya Wheway

'If it's to be, it's up to me.'

'Never mind whom you praise, but be very careful whom you blame.'

*'Spend less time worrying **who's** right, and more time deciding **what's** right.'*

H. Jackson Brown, Jr

BLAME

You must have met those people who love to blame others, whether it be their parents, boss, schooling, the Government or even the weather! Blame will hold you back. If you refuse to take responsibility for your actions, you will be unable to move on. Starting to develop a '*the buck stops here*' attitude and acknowledging responsibility for who you are and what happens to you can be daunting, but it is only by doing this that you can take charge of your life and direct its course.

BRAINSTORMING

This is a great technique for finding solutions to problems or creating strategies for achieving goals. It can be done on your own or in a small group, but the benefit of a group is that you will have more resources to hand and ideas spark off each other. Start from the basis that anything is possible.

1 Take a pen and a large piece of blank paper.
2 Draw a circle in the middle and in it write a few
   words which describe what you are aiming to achieve.
3 Without pausing to think too much, write down words
   or phrases that describe possible ideas for solving the
   problem. Don't reject any ideas, no matter what the
   obstacles may seem.
4 When you have exhausted all ideas, fold the paper
   up and put it away for a day or two.
5 Return to your brainstorm sheet and pull out the
   key ideas. Brainstorm on how you could get these
   to work, rather than dwelling on reasons why they
   might not work, and note down your action plan.

*'Positive people say it may be difficult, but it's
possible, whereas negative people say it may be
possible but it's too difficult.'*

*'A bend in the road is not the end of the road ...
unless you fail to make the turn.'*

*'An invasion of armies can be resisted, but not an
idea whose time has come.'*

Victor Hugo

*'If you always do what you always did, you'll always
get what you always got ... so if you want something
different, guess what you've got to do? Change!'*

*'You cannot change anyone. No one can change
you. You can change you. And if you do you'll find
the world changes with you.'*

CHANGE

It is true that the only person we can change is ourselves, but it is also true that while we cannot change anyone else, we can either bring out the best or the worst in them.

We crave balance, certainty and security. Yet one of the only things we can be sure of is change, which challenges our ability to live in harmony, particularly if it is unwanted and comes as a shock. Help lies in adjusting our perception of the changes that are happening and will happen. Yet again, focusing on the positive is our salvation. Some changes you can anticipate – in which case prepare yourself for the feelings you may experience, work out strategies for coping and develop a plan of action. Sometimes we need to initiate change ourselves in order to improve a situation. This too can be scary, but planning and courage give control and confidence.

'It is never too late to re-examine our choices.
Re-examination is wise. We always have choices.'
Anne Wilson Schaef

CHOICES

We often use language that tells us we have no choices: 'I must do ... I have to ... I've got to ...'. In fact there is only one thing that we all have to do, and that is to die. The rest of our life is up to us. There are three reasons why we choose to do anything: first, because it gives us pleasure; secondly, because we have not got the courage to do anything else; thirdly, because not doing it would give us a guilty conscience.

No one's life is perfect, so make the decisions that are best for you overall, and once you have made your decision, go for it wholeheartedly and make it work to the best of your ability. We *can* choose to be happy or unhappy, kind or unkind, to be as healthy as we can or to undermine our health, to enjoy life or to treat it as a trial. Don't be one of those who lives their life 'if only ...'

'Remember not only to say the right thing in the right place, but – far more difficult still – to leave unsaid the wrong thing at the tempting moment!'

'We have been given two ears and one mouth. Use them in that order.'

COMMUNICATION

What we say is not as important as making people understand what we mean, and understanding what other people mean. Major problems in relationships occur through breakdown in communication, so to avoid this:

- Don't bottle your feelings up. If you would like someone to know something, tell them: don't expect them to be a mindreader.
- Hone your listening skills: ask questions first to avoid jumping to the wrong conclusions, and ask others how they read the situation.
- Remember that knowledge can be power when it is *not* shared.
- Remember that we all have a right to our own opinions and others have a right to theirs.
- Do not allow important conversations to be interrupted by the phone.
- One of the most valuable things you can give another person is 100% of your attention.

CONCENTRATION

Akin to meditation, active concentration means focusing on one object and seeing all parts of it clearly and minutely, without being distracted by anything else.

The exercise below will help you to develop your concentration abilities, which in turn will enable you to see things more clearly, solve problems or use time more effectively.

You will need peace and quiet and to be sitting in a comfortable position. The object you concentrate on should be simple: for example, a candle, a flower or a vegetable.

1 Gaze firmly at the object, with your body remaining relaxed.
2 Gently bring your mind back if it wanders.
3 Blink when you want to, and continue for 1 minute at first, going up to 5 minutes with more practice.

CREATIVITY

As a result of negative programming most of us are unaware of the extent of our creative abilities. Often I ask groups if they believe they cannot paint and draw, and most people will raise their hands. When I ask them when they last tried, the answer is invariably 'at school'.

Many of us have limited ourselves through life bocause of a negative experience many years ago. It may be that we had a poor teacher, or that we had no interest in the subject, or that we had drawn something and been mocked.

Start unleashing your hidden creative powers and encourage their development. Listen to your dreams, make up stories for your children instead of reading to them, doodle and experiment with poetry. Embark on a weekend or nightschool course for painting, pottery or jewellery making. Have a go!

'Help me never to judge another until I have walked a day in his steps.'

'A fault mender is better than a fault finder.'

'Don't forget, a person's greatest emotional need is to feel appreciated.'

H. Jackson Brown, Jr

'Give compliments frequently; receive them graciously.'
Tanya Wheway

'If you manage a team of people, regularly go out of your office and actively look for people doing something right, and tell them.'

Ken Blanchard

CRITICISM

We remember criticisms and insults for years; whereas compliments stay with us only a short time. You need to give at least three times as many compliments as criticisms for them to equalize. Watch yourself, and see how easy it is to be critical without realizing it. If you do need to criticize an adult, think first of the positive outcome you want and do some preparation so you can lead the conversation to that conclusion. Don't lecture, but ask questions so that you encourage understanding, acceptance and committment. Trying to make the other person feel bad will not achieve anything, so instead empathize with their feelings and be specific and realistic in your requests.

If you are on the receiving end, calmly agree with the truth in the criticism, if there is any, or calmly acknowledge that there *may* be some truth in the criticism, and ask for clarification. Thank the person for their feedback and look objectively at what you can learn from it.

DELEGATION

'Don't hesitate, delegate!'

Delegation can keep your sanity. If you are one of those people who knows no one can do the job as well as you can, you are probably overloaded with work and spend a lot of time huffing and puffing about it. I personally am not a very good delegator, but I recognize that if I have made the decision to do something myself I should do it with a good grace. You can get family members to help more by rewarding them for the things they do and withdrawing services for the things they don't, rather than just nagging and moaning.

DOGS AND WHAT THEY TEACH US

♥ When loved ones come home, always run to greet them.
♥ Take naps and stretch before rising.
♥ Eat with gusto and enthusiasm.
♥ When someone is having a bad day, be silent, sit close by and nuzzle them gently.
♥ Delight in the simple joy of a nice long walk.
♥ When you're happy, dance around and wag your entire body.

'Tread softly because you tread on my dreams.'

W. B. Yeats

'If you can dream it, you can do it.'

Walt Disney

'You see things and you say "Why?" But I dream
things that never were: and say, "Why not?"'

G. B. Shaw

'If you have built castles in the air, your work need
not be lost; that is where they should be. Now put
the foundations underneath them.'

Henry Thoreau

DREAMS

Many people believe that dreams hold the key to the past or the future. Others use them as a way of understanding the present. Scientists and artists often keep a notepad next to their beds in order to jot down ideas and solutions that come to them in dreams, or in the period just before sleep when the mind is relaxed. It is said that Einstein came to his theory of relativity in this way. Dreams are another way of visualizing your future goals: compare Disney and Shaw's beliefs with those of Lord Kelvin, who said in 1885, 'Heavier than air, flying machines are impossible.'

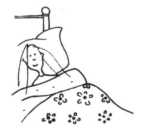

'*Children have more need of role models than critics.*'
Carolyn Coats

ENCOURAGEMENT

Lead by example: don't expect people to listen to what you say and ignore what you do. Look for opportunities to give positive feedback, offer help of a practical nature, send a beautiful card with a few kind words carefully chosen and encourage others to demonstrate their support.

'Excellence is the result of high intention, sincere effort, intelligent direction and skilful execution: it represents the wise choice of many alternatives.'

EXCELLENCE

When I was young and foolish I was 'conned' into selling magazines from door to door. My manager was quite a gangster, but I did learn one thing of value from him: 'Aim for the stars, and you will live in the penthouse; aim for the penthouse and you will live in the gutter.' You will achieve so much more If you stretch yourself and refuse to accept second best.

Excellence can be attained if you:

☆ care more than others think is wise
☆ risk more than others think is safe
☆ dream more than others think is practical
☆ expect more than others think is possible
☆ never take no for an answer
☆ don't let rejection deter you
☆ expect the best and believe that you deserve the best
☆ put all your resourcefulness behind those things you *really* want.

'*Mens sana in corpore sano.*'

Latin proverb

'*If you don't use it, you lose it.*'

EXERCISE — YOUR BODY

Mind and body are inextricably linked, and we cannot develop our minds without stretching our bodies. There is no need to push yourself too far, but moderate exercise such as fast walking, gardening, swimming, a quick work-out, even housework if you do it with gusto, all give your mind a chance to recharge itself, alleviate the harmful effects of stress and release any tension that has built up. By taking exercise we redress our body's balance and usually find that we generate more mental and physical energy and greater creativity – for by leaving your thoughts alone you create space for them to come up with new ideas.

'You are never too old to learn.'

'To be interesting we need to be interested.'

EXERCISE — YOUR MIND

We all know the feeling of stagnation if we have been too involved in childcare, housework or mundane tasks to pay attention to our intellectual life. You feel you're getting old if your memory starts to go, but you can ginger it up by being interested in lots of things and never stopping learning. Indeed, I once had a lady of 82 who came on an assertiveness course!

A few simple things you could do are:

- Take up drawing to sharpen up your observation of detail.
- Read a newspaper every day.
- Do the crossword.
- Patronize your local library.
- Enrol on a new course.

'If you try you might, if you don't you won't.'

'What would you attempt to do if you knew you could not fail?'

FAILURE

There was once a famous American:
He failed in business in '31.
He ran as a state legislator and lost in '32.
He tried business again in '33 and failed again.
His sweetheart died in '35.
He had a nervous breakdown in '36.
He ran for state elector in '40, after he regained
his health.
He was defeated for Congress in '43, defeated again
for Congress in '48, defeated when he ran for the
Senate in '55, and defeated for vice presidency of
the US in '56.
He ran for the Senate again in '58 and lost.
This man never quit. He kept on trying 'til the last.
In 1869, this man, Abraham Lincoln, was elected
President of the United States.

'Feel the fear and do it anyway.'

Susan Jeffers

'Courage is a kind of salvation.'

Plato

'The only thing we have to fear is fear itself.'

Roosevelt

'You can do what you want, if you don't think you can't, so don't think you can't, think you can.'

M. Cou

'Don't be afraid to take a big step if one is indicated. You can't cross a chasm in two small jumps.'

David Lloyd George

FEAR

A certain amount of fear can be life-preserving, but often our fear just leads to procrastination and inactivity. Fear focuses on imaginary, negative, *what if* scenarios, and immobilizes us. When we are children we have little fear but no skills. As adults we have the abilities and skills, but have developed a sense of fear which holds us back.

- Identify your fears and rationalize them by writing them down and verbalizing how you feel.
- Write down all the things you miss out on by allowing your fear to dominate. Also write down the good things you could do, achieve and experience if you were able to let go of your fear.
- Decide to take control of yourself and your fate.
- What is the worst that might happen? Is it really all that bad?
- What is the best that might happen?
- Choose bravery and risk it. Coping with fear starts NOW.

FUN

In a society that functions on competition and productivity, seeking fun is often regarded as immature or self-indulgent. In fact, fun, laughter and happiness make life more rewarding for ourselves and those around us, and enhance our immune system. As we get older and take on more responsibilities we risk taking ourselves too seriously. As a Hawaiian friend of mine says, 'Hang loose man, hang loose.'

- Watch more comedy shows, go to a musical, a funfair or a pantomime with children.
- Play with the kids.
- Don't take yourself too seriously.
- Cultivate fun people as friends.
- Fly a kite.
- Learn some clean funny jokes.
- Be spontaneous.
- Giggle.
- Do something just for the fun of it (people love having a go on our swing at The Sanctuary).

'People rarely succeed at anything unless they have fun doing it.'

'Good humour is very inexpensive. It is one of the pleasures in life that is relatively free.'
Anne Wilson Schaef

'Joking is undignified: that is why it is good for one's soul.'
G. K. Chesterton

'Perhaps one has to be very old before one learns how to be amused rather than shocked.'
Pearl S. Buck

'It's the good girls who keep the diaries – the bad girls never have the time.'

'The starting point of all achievement is desire. Keep this constantly in mind. Weak desires bring weak results, just as a small amount of fire makes a small amount of heat.'

Napoleon Hill

'I can't *never did anything*, I will try *has worked wonders*, and I will do *will perform miracles*.'

'Obstacles are those frightful things you see when you take your eyes off the goal.'

GOALS

Goals give purpose and direction to our lives. Write down your main goals in life – I would suggest 'health' and 'happiness' – then write your secondary goals underneath. These can include anything from getting married to becoming a millionaire. The main thing is to check that your secondary goals lead you towards your main goals. Remember that the journey is as important as the destination: the former may account for many years in your life, whereas the latter may only be a moment in time. When setting goals for yourself, remember that they must be SMART, ie:

- ◎ **s**pecific
- ◎ **m**easurable
- ◎ **a**chievable
- ◎ **r**ealistic
- ◎ **t**ime-based.

They should also be reviewed from time to time to meet changing circumstances and changes within ourselves.

GUILT

It is one thing to be truly sorry for a past action or inaction, but carrying around a load of guilt does not do anyone any good, and can even do you and those close to you harm. There is nothing you can do to change the past. Absolutely nothing. Do not use guilty feelings as an excuse to berate yourself and don't waste time on self-indulgent regret. Say sorry if you can, and do something to help if you can. Then forgive yourself. Try to use mistakes as learning experiences in order to grow from them and avoid similar situations in the future.

The Guilt Game, identified by Dr Wayne Dyer, is called a game because it is played by two people, and if one of them refuses to play, it becomes null and void. There are people who use guilt to manipulate and control. Be strong and refuse to play the game. Say, for example, 'I want to have a good, positive relationship with you, but I am not going to be manipulated by you; I will not play the Guilt Game. I will do such and such but it needs to be on terms which we both feel good about.'

'There is luxury in self-reproach. When we blame ourselves we feel no one else has the right to blame us.'
Oscar Wilde

'Show me a woman who doesn't feel guilty and I'll show you a man.'

Erica Jong

'Happiness is not having what you want, but wanting what you have.'

'The three great essentials of happiness are: something to do, someone to love, and something to hope for.'

'Most people are about as happy as they make up their minds to be.'

Abraham Lincoln

'When one door of happiness closes, another opens; but often we look so long at the closed door that we do not see the one which has been opened for us.'

Helen Keller

'Perfection is an elusive butterfly. When we cease to demand perfection, the business of being happy becomes that much easier.'

HAPPINESS

Some people are so fixed on goals (achieving money, position, power, 'things') that they forget to enjoy the journey. These people are in the 'I'll be happy when ...' trap, and the danger of this is that when these goals are achieved they are left with a feeling of Emptiness; or if things go wrong, say if a marriage breaks down, they ignore the many good things they have had along the way: the things they have learned, the people they have met, the happy times they have had or the children they have reared.

When people are happy they have fewer 'wants' and are therefore more inclined to help others. It is also now well-documented that happiness is linked in a physical way to health: laughing, for instance, releases endorphins and other substances that enhance our immune systems. Happiness is not about pretending everything is fine when it clearly is not. It is about shifting the balance of what you are focusing on. Seek out the silver lining and count your blessings. The time to be happy is now.

HYPNOSIS AND SELF-HYPNOSIS

Practised therapeutically, hypnosis is a very effective method of inducing a deep state of relaxation (not sleep, and not unconsciousness) in which positive suggestions can be introduced into the mind. With repetition these suggestions gradually take root and become a part of your life. Hypnosis can help with the healing of anxiety and addictions and improve confidence.

You can practise hypnotherapy on yourself by using one of the exercises on pp101–102 to enter a profound state of relaxation, then repeat the affirmations you have selected as appropriate for you (*see p3*). Don't expect instant results, but gradually over time you will find you are better able to achieve the things you want.

'Once you label me, you negate me.'

Sören Kierkegaard

'What is he?
A man, of course.
Yes, but what does he do?
He lives and is a man.'

D. H. Lawrence

LABELS

Almost from the moment a child is born we are compelled to label it. 'He's so good', 'She's very demanding', and so on. As children grow up we start handing out labels like 'You're bad/stupid/selfish/clumsy'. We don't really mean this: it is not the child that is bad, but what they did that was bad – quite different. If you keep telling a child that they are stupid or clumsy you are encouraging the child to grow up with erroneous beliefs about themselves. Far better to say, 'What you did was an idiotic thing – which is a shame, because you're very bright,' thereby reinforcing the good in the child.

When we meet people we want to label them according to their job or social status, rather than as a human being. We even give ourselves labels: 'I'm shy', 'I'm forgetful', 'I'm no good at figures.' The repetition of this in our mind prevents us from changing. Instead, use positive labels (*see also Affirmations p3, Change p23, Choices p25, Language p62 and Programming p96*).

LANGUAGE

What we say, whether it be to ourselves (out loud, or silently in our heads, known as self-talk) or to others, has a powerful effect on what we think, feel and believe. If we constantly use negative words such as 'can't' 'won't' 'shouldn't' 'don't', we convince ourselves that the world is a harsh, difficult place and we alienate others who simply do not wish to be surrounded by moaners.

Really listen to what you say throughout a whole day, particularly registering anything you say that might be negative or not the real truth. Then turn the words around. Don't say 'I feel terrible'. Say 'I could feel better'. Don't say 'I'm too old to do that', say 'I'm still young enough to give that a go'. Instead of saying 'My child can't do maths,' say 'My child could use some extra help with maths'. Often if we say we 'can't' do something, what we really mean is that we don't want to do it, or haven't yet learnt. Then say so. Tell the truth. Positive language will make you feel far better!

'You tend to believe what you tell yourself, especially if you say it often enough.'

'The one important thing I've learned over the years is the difference between taking one's work seriously and one's self seriously. The first is imperative and the second is disasterous.'

Dame Margot Fonteyn

'Laughter is the best medicine.'

LAUGHTER

Norman Cousins, author of *Anatomy of an Illness*, was informed he had an incurable disease. He believed that his serious approach to life had brought about his illness and that the opposite could provide the cure. So he hired funny films, which he watched for a number of hours a day – and, much to the astonishment of his physicians, he laughed himself well.

According to Dr John Hart, a bio-medical researcher who studies laughter, laughing releases endorphins in the brain, which gives the body a natural 'high', relieves pain, tones up the heart, boosts the Immune system, reduces stress and burns off calories. He reports that ten seconds of good belly-laughing is equivalent to ten minutes rowing when it comes to raising the heart rate. As children we laugh around 400 times a day, but by the time we are adults we can only squeeze out 15 good giggles

LEARNING

'Instead of using the words "if only", try substituting the words, "next time".'

'Everything that irritates us about others can lead us to an understanding of ourselves.'

Carl Jung

*'What I hear I forget
What I see I remember
What I do I know.'*

It is never too late to learn. We should continue to learn until the day we go to meet our maker. I rather like the definition of an 'expert': an 'ex' is a has-been and a 'spurt' is a drip under pressure. People can be specialists, but it is highly unlikely that they know everything there is to know: there is always something new to learn. Remember to keep trying new things and seeking new experiences.

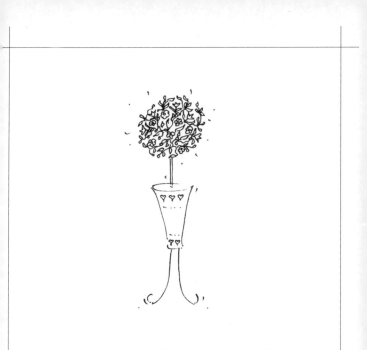

'Every person you meet knows something you don't:
learn from them.'

LUCK

The word 'luck' would be more aptly named 'opportunity'. It is a matter of keeping your eyes open, seeing it when it is out there, grabbing it with both hands, being determined to make it work, putting effort in and often taking risks. When we were 'restructured' out of Champneys and eventually returned again four years later as part owners, many of our loyal clientele put it down to luck, others to fate or justice. It was no such thing.

Blaming lack of luck for your own shortcomings is a comfort blanket holding you back. 'Luck' is a four-letter word: dump it and direct your own fate.

'It's funny how the harder I work, the luckier I get.'

'You make your own luck.'

'You will always miss 100% of the shots you don't take.'

'Luck is a matter of preparation meeting opportunity.'

'I believe that what a woman resents is not so much giving herself in pieces as giving herself purposelessly.'
Anne Morrow Lindbergh

'Martyrs are not much fun to live with. Do what you do with good grace, or don't do it. The sun will still rise and the sun will still set: you are not as indispensable as you think.'

Tanya Wheway

MARTYRDOM

If you are doing something you don't want to do, don't huff and puff and make a big song and dance about how generous and kind you are being. Do it with a good grace or learn to say no. Jennifer Louden recommends this assertiveness technique for 'getting in touch with your inner bitch': simply say 'I don't think so.' So much nicer than saying a flat 'no', yet just as firm.

MEDITATION

Meditation is an ideal antidote to stress, and has been found to calm the heart beat, lower blood pressure, soothe jangled nerves, boost the immune system and ease pain. It is mind, body and soul food, and the time out it gives you allows you to put more back into life. The point is to clear your mind of its constant jabbering commentary and concentrate on a single thing.

Beginner's Meditation Exercise

1. Sit in an upright but comfortable position. Close your eyes.
2. Breathe slowly and deeply.
3. Inhale, exhale and repeat 'A'. See the letter in your mind.
4. Inhale, exhale and repeat 'B'. Continue through the alphabet until you reach 'Z'.
5. Your mind will wander at first, but gently bring it back.
6. End your meditation with a few moments of stillness and slowly open your eyes.

'*Thoughts create intentions and intentions create reality.*'

MIND POWER

Homo sapiens appeared on Earth 3,500,000 years ago, but it was only 500 years ago that mankind discovered the location of the brain. Prior to this even Aristotle, quite rationally, believed that our brains were located in the heart and stomach area, because this is where we experienced the direct physical manifestation of mental activity most regularly and dramatically. The human brain is still in many respects a mystery. It is estimated that we only use between 1 and 10% of our brain's capacity. None the less our minds can achieve a tremendous amount.

Unfortunately our 'programming', the messages we receive from the outside world, from conception to birth, lead us to seriously underestimate what we can really achieve if we only put out minds to it. Use your mind effectively to the advantage of yourself and others. Appreciate it, nurture it, develop and direct it to be of use to you and anyone whose life you touch.

MUSIC AND SOUND THERAPY

In ancient times music was regarded as the speech of angels, and still today it has the unique ability to affect our moods and emotions. Music consists of rhythm and vibration – and so also do our bodies, for each cell resonates with its own frequency. When we are upset or angry we feel 'out of tune'; when we are happy we are 'on song'. Use the power of music to create real changes in your life. Choose what you listen to with care, and make sure it is going to have the desired soothing or energizing effect. Don't always use it as musical wallpaper, take the time to relax fully and listen actively to music.

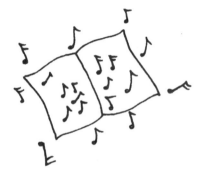

'Use your eyes as if tomorrow you would be stricken
blind. And use the same method for your other senses.'

Helen Keller

NEGATIVE THINKING

Misery is contagious. Make a list of all the negative people in your life, and don't spend time with them – making a distinction of course between the moaners and groaners and those who are really in need. Conversely, make a list of the upbeat, joyful people you know and make a point of seeing them more.

You can choose to wallow in negativity or change it. Listen to your own conversation for a couple of hours – you may be surprised at the amount of negative words and cynical phrases you are using. You can actually decide to be miserable, and you can decide not to be miserable. Try it. (*See also Affirmations p3, Attitude p13, Change p23, Choices p25, Positive Thinking p88 and Visualization p128.*)

'The strangest and most fantastic fact about negative emotions is that people actually worship them.'

P. D. Ouspensky

'People who deal in sunshine are the ones who draw the crowds. They always do more business than those who peddle clouds.'

'When I feel down I call it an attack of PLOMS disease. Poor Little Old Me. The antidote I find is to go out there and do something nice for someone, and it's amazing how that PLOMS disease disappears.'

Dame Edna Everage

'Never feel sorry for yourself: it's a sure way to misery.'

NLP

Neuro linguistic programming is a relatively new science that has developed from the discovery that people perceive and communicate in different ways. It focuses on how language, both verbal and non-verbal, affects our nervous system. When communicating we tend to use one element of our neurology – visual, auditory or kinesthetic – more than our other senses. A visual person will tend to see the world in pictures and this is reflected in their language ('I see'). An auditory person will focus on sounds and pepper their language with listening words, and a kinesthetic person will talk about feelings and touch. When we can communicate in the language that the receiver is in tune with we can achieve so much more.

NLP is a fascinating and useful subject and I recommend attending an introductory course on the subject.

'NLP is the science of how to run your brain in an optimal way to produce the results you desire.'
Anthony Robbins

'Don't major in minor things.'

H. Jackson Brown Jr

'Go some distance away, because the work appears smaller and more of it can be taken at a glance and lack of harmony or proportion is rapidly seen.'

Leonardo da Vinci

PERSPECTIVE

It is true that we often can't see the wood for the trees, that we could do with taking a step back and looking at the whole picture in a different way.

Take time out of your normal environment. Go on a course, whether it be connected with business, a hobby or something quite new. Spend a few days at a health farm or spiritual retreat. Try an outward-bound course, or simply stay in a quiet spot and walk, sleep, eat, read, listen to music and think. Whatever you do, take a notebook and write down anything interesting that comes into your head. You may find you have some headings for further action or contemplation. Make sure you do not lose what you have written and, within the next two weeks, take a few hours to review your list.

PLANNING

Once we have decided where we are travelling to we have to plan the route we are going to take. It is the same with life: you first determine the what and then work out the how. However, it's a well known fact that long-range planning never works. We almost always get to our goal through means other than the ones we wrote down carefully on our 'five year goals' list. So why plan? Because people without long-range plans seldom get to where they want to be. In short, a plan will get you to your goal, but not in the way you had planned. Keep your dream in mind, but be prepared not just to change horses midstream, but boats too.

Making a plan is easy. Decide your goal, and a time for achieving it, and break up the time in between now and then into definite actions. Remember, to think before you act is always advisable.

'You are young and useful at any age if you are still planning for tomorrow.'

'People don't plan to fail, they fail to plan.'

'It is better to look ahead and prepare than to look back and regret.'

'Perhaps the most important thing that has come out of my life is the discovery that if you prepare yourself at every point as well as you can, with whatever means you have, however meagre they may seem, you will be able to grasp opportunity for broader experience when it appears. Without preparation you cannot do it.'

Helena Rubenstein

*'The mind is its own place, and in itself
Can make a heaven of Hell, a hell out of Heaven.'*
Milton

POSITIVE MENTAL ATTITUDE

We are made up of two things. One is our genetic background, over which we have no control; the other is the experiences we have undergone since birth. These experiences leave marks on our psychological make-up: every single thing that we have ever seen, heard, tasted, smelt is all stored in the huge database of our subconscious mind, a reference library to which we refer many times a day. We form our opinions, make decisions, form prejudices upon it – live our lives by it, if you like – so it is very powerful stuff.

In computer terminology there is something known as GIGO – Garbage In, Garbage Out – in other words if you put garbage into a computer you will get a load of garbage out; and this happens in our lives. We have all, over the years, had some garbage fed into our computers. The good news is that we *can* reprogramme our minds (*see p96*) and replace our negative programming with positive thoughts.

POSITIVE THINKING

It is a fact that people who have learnt how to develop a positive mental attitude are more successful, happier and healthier than their miserable counterparts. In any given moment, there is ample evidence to prove that life is a bed of thorns or a garden of roses, and how we feel about life depends on where we place our attention, or what we focus on. If you look for disaster, you will find it. But if you always try to focus on the positive, enjoy each moment and plan constructively and enthusiastically for the future, you may find you can effect a revolution in your life.

'We are not interested in the possibilities of defeat.'
                                                    Queen Victoria

'Keep looking up. Remember there is only mud
under your feet.'

'What your mind can conceive
that you will believe
your body can achieve.'

'The way I see it, if you want the rainbow you've got
to put up with the rain.'
                                                    Dolly Parton

'A child comes into the world as true potential.'

'Use what talents you possess: the woods would be very silent if no birds sang there except those that sang best.'

'There are hazards in everything one does but greater hazards in doing nothing.'

Shirley Williams

'If we did the things we are capable of doing, we would literally astound ourselves.'

POTENTIAL

Most of us go to our graves having no more than scratched the surface of our potential. If there is something you say you would like to do, then follow your dream and make it a reality. Stretch yourself, not just in the big things, but in the small things too. Have the courage to spread your wings.

PROBLEMS

It is important to get our 'problems' into perspective.
I have noticed that people do what I call 'horribleize' –
not a proper word I know, but very descriptive. They
exaggerate, call small nuisances disasters, tragedies, night-
mares, catastrophes. I once heard a speaker recommend
substituting these words with one word: 'inconvenient'.
Use your language to help you keep your perspective.

'There are positive problems and there are negative problems. A positive problem is when you pay too much tax, and a negative problem is when you don't have enough food to eat to live. Most of our problems in the developed countries are positive ones.'

Alan Wheway

'Do not say with regard to anything "I will do that tomorrow."'

The Koran

'Live your life so that your epitaph can read, "No regrets."'

PROCRASTINATION

'There's no time like the present.' 'Prevaricating can be boring, depressing and frustrating not only for ourselves, but also for those around us. Do you really want to do something – learn to tango, write a book, go gliding? – or do you just want to talk about it? If you do really want to do it, then work out exactly what, how, when, where and if there is a 'who' other than yourself, and DO IT… Alternatively, be honest with yourself and accept that you are not going to do it, and then move on.

PROGRAMMING FOR SUCCESS

'If a child lives with criticism, he learns to condemn
If a child lives with hostility, he learns to fight
If a child lives with ridicule, he learns to be shy
If a child lives with shame, he learns to be guilty
If a child lives with tolerance, he learns to be patient
If a child lives with encouragement, he learns
confidence
If a child lives with praise, he learns to appreciate
If a child lives with fairness, he learns justice
If a child lives with security, he learns to have faith
If a child lives with approval, he learns to like
himself
If a child lives with acceptance and friendship,
he learns to find love in the world.'

Anon

Think of instances in your life where you have accepted false and negative messages about yourself, and the impact it has had. The good news is that the past does not have to dictate the future. You can control what you do, say, think and feel. You can dump the garbage you have accumulated and reprogramme your mind. Remember, 'We are not what we think we are, but what we think, we are.'

The American saying 'What's the bottom line?' is a start. Ask yourself whether what you're doing, saying, thinking and feeling is giving positive or negative results. If the bottom line is negative, then surely it would make sense to see if we can change it. In order to do this three things are essential:

🍃 You must want to change. Really want to, not just have a vague feeling that it would be quite nice if…

🍃 You must believe in your ability. Think about yourself doing something positive and knowing you can.

🍃 Finally, a good old 'E' for effort. Nothing is achieved without this, and here we are back at 'want' and 'bottom line' again.

'Personally I think if a woman hasn't met the right man by the time she's 24, she may be lucky.'

Deborah Carr

In my book, the most important things in life are health, time and relationships. But the first two would be worth little without the third.

Tanya Wheway

'Whenever you want to marry someone, go have lunch with his ex-wife.'

Shelly Winters

RELATIONSHIPS

The longest and most important relationship you will ever have is with yourself. Good relationships with other people rest on the strength of our relationship with ourselves. Most of us were not brought up to love ourselves but to put others first and ourselves last: to be seen and not heard. But it is not selfish to be self-caring; having respect for yourself is not the same as being conceited. Start to build your self-esteem (*see p112*), the relationship you have with yourself, and your relationships with others will blossom.

Treasure and nurture all the relationships that are important to you: now. Tomorrow may be too late.

'Getting people to like you is only the other side of liking them.'

'People are lonely because they build walls instead of bridges.'

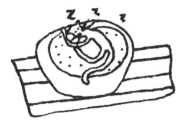

'If your mind is empty, it is always ready for anything; it is open to everything. In the beginner's mind there are many possibilities, in the expert's mind there are few.'

Shunryu Suzuki-Roshi

RELAXATION

When your mind is relaxed you will be in a more receptive state to absorb positive affirmations. You will also help to heal the damage caused by stress, and recharge your batteries.

Relaxation I
1 Raise your hands to your face.
2 Place your thumbs in your ears and gently place your index finger on your closed eyelids.
3 Put your middle fingers on either side of your nose.
4 Put your little fingers at the sides of your mouth.
5 Breathe lightly and turn your focus within.

Relaxation II

1 Sit or lie down in a comfortable position, with your body open.
2 Breathe slowly and deeply.
3 Focus your attention on the top of your head, tense the muscles and release.
4 Focus your attention on your forehead, tense the muscles and release.
5 Focus your attention on your eyelids, tense them and release.
6 Continue down your body, tensing and releasing the muscles of your body gently, feeling the tension ebb away as you go.
7 Try not to fall asleep, as you will gain more benefit if your mind is alert (although if you want to fall asleep, this is a good way to do it).
8 Come out of the relaxation gently.

Instant Relaxers

1. Shrug your shoulders, hold them in tension, and release.
2. Extend your legs, clench your feet and toes, and release.
3. Leave the room and take time to collect your thoughts.

RESOURCES

We all have limited resources, so spend your time, energy, mind, body and spirit wisely. Make a list of those whom you want to give your resources to.

Relationship self	Work self	Individual self
Immediate family	Paid work	Physical
Extended family	Housework	Intellectual
Friends	Voluntary work	Emotional
Associates		Spiritual

Work out what percentage of your time you spend on the different aspects of yourself and see if you have the balance right. You don't have to divide your time evenly, and the percentage of time you spend on each 'self' will change throughout your life. But if you feel the balance is not right, give some thought as to how you might redress the balance. When all three selves are functioning they feed and support each other. If, however, you have put all your 'egos' into one basket you are in danger of going under.

'Like a bank account, you can't keep spending out, without putting something back in … or your account dries up and you become irritable and not much fun to be around.'

Tanya Wheway

'If it's to be, it's up to me.'

'I believe that a judicious mixture of hard work, clear thinking, humour and self-confidence are the ingredients of effective living. I do not believe in fancy formulas or historical excursions into your past to discover you were "harshly toilet trained" and that someone else is responsible for your unhappiness.'

Dr Wayne Dyer

RESPONSIBILITY

Stand up and be accountable for your own actions – or inactions. Only by doing this can you take charge of your own life rather than acting as a puppet dancing to others' tunes, or blaming all and sundry for the lack of good things in your life. The world isn't fair, it isn't just and your own fate is largely up to you.

RIGHT AND LEFT BRAINS

The two hemispheres of our brains have different functions. The left side, which controls the right side of the body, is concerned with numbers, logic, analysis and reasoning. The right side is connected with creativity, imagination, rhythm, colour, humour and dreams. Our society values the functions of the left side over those of the right, but for our bodies and lives to be in balance we need to develop the capacities of our right brain. You may remember at school you were told to 'stop daydreaming and do your sums' – the world of analysis and statistics is all very well, but where would we be without vision, gut feeling and passion?

'Risk and reward travel side by side. Avoid one and the other will also pass you by.'

'You cannot discover new oceans unless you have the courage to lose sight of the shore.'

RISK

There are, of course, risks and risks. There are dare-devil types who enjoy flirting with danger and get a kick out of putting themselves at risk. This is quite different from taking calculated risks, not for risk's sake, but to achieve goals which are important to us.

> 'To laugh is to risk appearing a fool
> To weep is to risk appearing sentimental
> To reach out for another is to risk involvement
> To expose feelings is to risk rejection
> To place your dreams before the crowd is to risk ridicule
> To love is to risk not being loved in return
> To go forward in the face of overwhelming odds is to risk failure.
> The person who risks nothing does nothing, has nothing and is nothing. Only a person who takes risks is free.'

SELF-ESTEEM

*'If you really do put a small value upon yourself,
rest assured that the world will not raise the price.'*

*'Remember, no one can make you feel inferior
without your consent.'*

Eleanor Roosevelt

Self-esteem is the inner picture we have of ourselves, complete with what we see as 'good' and 'bad' points. It affects the way we relate to others, the choices we make and what we think we are capable of achieving. A poor self-image may have been fostered over the years by our experiences and by what people have said to us. Low self-esteem leads to a spiral of negative thinking which in turn leads us to negative, self-defeating behaviour. Many subjects in this book will help you build a more positive relationship with yourself, but the following list is a good starting point.

- ✤ Challenge your thinking. Stop yourself, and ask 'Is this really true?'
- ✤ Be kind to yourself and respect yourself.
- ✤ Face up to your fears.
- ✤ Look for the positive in your situation.
- ✤ Be your own best friend: give yourself good advice.
- ✤ Make a list of your attributes and qualities.
- ✤ Create special affirmations for yourself (*see p3*).
- ✤ Think of those things about yourself you would like to – and can – change (*see Brainstorming p20 and Planning p84*).
- ✤ Go on an assertiveness course.

> *'Whenever I dwell for any length of time on my own shortcomings, they gradually begin to seem mild, harmless, rather engaging little things.'*
>
> Margaret Halsey

SERENITY

Peacefulness, graciousness, gracefulness, calmness, reflection, contentment, tranquillity, stillness, serenity: how often are these part of our lives? Most of us rush through life at a mighty rate of knots, rarely stopping to smell the flowers. I too try to pack too much into every day, and writing this series of books has reminded me to pay attention to some of the things I have let slip or that have got out of balance. I can feel a New Year's resolution coming on and it is only August! You might like to dip into the *Spirit* book to discover new ways of achieving serenity in your life.

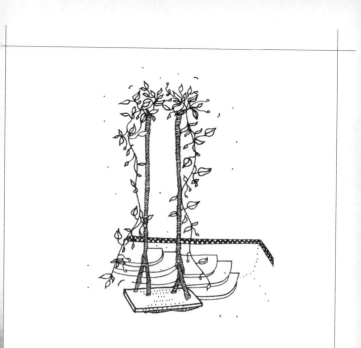

'Always behave like a duck. Keep calm and unruffled on the surface, but paddle like the devil underneath.'

'In the race to be better or best, do not miss the joy of being.'

'When you bring in something new, get rid of something old.'

Elaine St James

'Use the KISS principle: Keep It Simple, Silly.'

SIMPLICITY

How much space in your house is taken up with clothes you never wear, old letters, piles of photos, old school books, out-of-date magazines, broken toys, rarely used exercise equipment, and things you are hanging on to just in case you might need them one day? Whether you realize it or not, your clutter is weighing you down, preventing you from moving through life cleanly and clearly. Don't worry, you don't have to get rid of *every-thing*, just start the great chuck-out process now – you will feel liberated and renewed. Not only that – your unwanted stuff may be perfect for car boot sales, local charities or schools.

Many of us have a tendency to over-complicate our lives. I have heard that it is a Japanese custom to keep beautiful possessions in a cupboard, and display only one at a time in order to enjoy it fully. Keep the KISS principle in mind and apply it to your daily life.

SMILE

'It costs nothing, but creates much.
It enriches those who receive without impoverishing
those who give.
It happens in a flash yet the memory of it lasts forever.
None are so rich they can get along without it, and
none so poor but are richer for its benefits.
It creates happiness in the home, fosters goodwill in
business and is the countersign of friends.
It is rest for the weary, daylight to the discouraged,
sunshine to the sad and nature's best antidote for
trouble.
Yet it cannot be bought, begged, borrowed or stolen,
for it is no earthly use to anyone unless it is given away.
And if in the course of the day some of your friends are
too tired to give you a smile, why don't you give them
one of yours?
For nobody needs a smile so much as those who have
none left to give!'

SPONTANEITY

'Analysis kills spontaneity. The grain, once ground into flour, springs and germinates no more.'
Henri Frederic Amiel

It is wonderful to have goals, to plan and prepare, and to have some order and structure in your life. But watch that you do not become too rigid and routine-bound. If someone you enjoy being with suddenly says 'Let's go to Paris this weekend,' don't look for all the reasons you need to think about it, plan and prepare for it … just throw some things in a case and do it. Hang loose, be spontaneous, do something just for the *heluv* it!

STOP!

If you are overwhelmed with problems, take some time out to reflect and distance yourself from your pain. This is not an easy exercise, but persistence with it will pay off.

♥ What are my **S**trengths?
♥ What is this problem trying to **T**each me?
♥ What **O**pportunities come with this problem?
♥ What are the potential **P**ositives?

STRENGTHS AND WEAKNESSES

'Don't try to put square pegs in round holes.'

Everyone has both, yet it is in itself a strength to be aware of your own strengths and weaknesses. Sadly many people only seem to be able to see their weaknesses while others only see their strengths.

Take a piece of paper and think quietly about your strengths and weaknesses, remembering that a weakness in one circumstance may become a strength in another. Look at your strengths and decide how you might use them better for the benefit of yourself and others. Look at your weaknesses and identify those it would be good to change, improve and develop, and explore how you might do that. If there are any weaknesses you feel you can't change, admit them and structure your life to make the most of your strengths.

STRESS

'For peace of mind, resign as general manager of the universe.'

'When things go wrong, treat yourself right!'
Robert Holden

Stress is now recognized by the medical and healing professions as a serious problem. Some stress is avoidable, so avoid it if you can. The rest is unavoidable, so we need to learn how to control our reaction to it. If you are stuck in a traffic jam and are late for an appointment, there is nothing you can do to make the cars go faster, so you can choose whether to get frustrated and angry, or whether to do something constructive: listen to a tape, plan a project, prepare a speech, phone a friend or blow bubbles. See the time as a gift to you to fill with something worthwhile.

Of course some pressure is good for us: it relieves boredom and it helps performance. But if we go beyond our optimal stress level we put ourselves in grave danger. A stressful situation sets off a string of hormonal reactions in our bodies which cause us harm. Hormones such as adrenalin and cortisol are released, our blood rushes away from our stomach, our vessels constrict, our metabolism speeds up, our muscles tense and our heartbeat races ... all to aid us in our flight or fight. We don't work this 'stuff' off in a physical sense as we might have done in prehistoric times, so it remains in our bodies and damages the immune system, leaving an underlying sense of anxiety and depression and making us vulnerable to illness. Learning to relax, release and let go of stress is an essential part of learning to live in harmony and peace, but better still is not to get stressed in the first place. In this little book are exercises and ideas that will start to help you restore inner calm and help you control the stress life lays upon you.

SUCCESS

'Judge your success by the degree that you are enjoying peace, health and love.'

Jackson

"A hundred years from now it will not matter what my bank account was, the sort of house I lived in, or the kind of car I drove ... but the world may be different because I was important in the life of a child.'

'Gather up the past and invest it in the future.'

'Success is a journey, not a destination.'

First you need to define what success means for you. How will you judge, when it is time to move on, whether you and the life you have lived have been successful? Be guided in your decisions by your values, your relationships and your dreams, holding on to what you believe in most.

'Success is not something real – you cannot touch it or cuddle it as you can your loved ones.'

TIME MANAGEMENT

*'Waste of time is the most extravagant and costly
of all expenses.'*

'Today is not a dress rehearsal for tomorrow.'

*'Yesterday is a cancelled cheque; tomorrow is a
promissory note: today is the only cash you have –
so spend it wisely.'*

Kay Lyons

If you feel you could use more time in the week, make
a weekly time log, keeping a record of what you do each
hour. Identify the things you found frustrating and time-
wasting, and see if you can work out better ways of doing
them. To encourage yourself, think about what you would
like to spend the extra time you will save doing. Make
sure that in the time you spend with your loved ones you
are giving yourself 100%. Time-saving ideas include:

- ⏱ Touch a piece of paper only once, then file it, bin it or pass it on.
- ⏱ Be tidy and organized. A little time spent at the end of each day tidying your desk will save hours looking for lost papers. The same goes for drawers and cupboards, pockets and bags.
- ⏱ Learn to delegate.
- ⏱ Use a mobile or hands-free phone if you spend a lot of time travelling.
- ⏱ Prioritize your to-do list.
- ⏱ Do the hard things first.
- ⏱ Have a voice-mail system.
- ⏱ Get cooperation from your family with household tasks.

VISUALIZATION

*'Somehow these mental techniques restore
intelligence by operating from the mind's awareness.
It is one intelligence in our bodies speaking to
another and bringing it back to normal.'*

Deepak Chopra

Mental images are constantly flooding through your brain, and these pictures have a profound effect on your entire system: physically, mentally, emotionally and spiritually, and they have the power to harm or heal you.

Visualization is taught by complementary health practitioners as a way of harnessing the power of imagery for good. Phobia sufferers imagine themselves confronting their fears and surviving, cancer sufferers picture their healthy cells overcoming the cancerous cells. Shy people see themselves as happy and confident. Constantly bringing to mind 'as if' pictures will help your body and mind bring the reality about.

Visualization is also used as a tool for successful living in the material sense. Make up a scrapbook with pictures clipped from magazines which show your ideal life: a certain type of car, house, garden, job, children, for example. Refine and develop your scrapbook over time and see yourself living the life you desire. Many people testify to the remarkable power of this technique, which focuses the mind on creating the life you want.

When you are reprogramming your mind, go through each sense in the following order:

1 Sound: *speak* the affirmation aloud.
2 Visualization: *see* yourself achieving your goals.
3 Imagine how you would *feel*.
4 Imagine the *smells* and *taste*, the fine details of the experience.

The most effective time for this is when your mind is relaxed, either first thing in the morning or last thing at night. It can also be used to imagine a successful outcome of a previously embarrassing experience.

'To be successful in business it's good to have a brain, but it's essential to have a strong stomach and feet that move.'

'Success is 10% inspiration and 90% perspiration.'

'Some people dream of worthy accomplishments, whilst others stay awake and do them.'

'Passion is powerful ... nothing was ever achieved without it, and nothing can take its place. No matter what you face in life, if your passion is great enough, you will find the strength to succeed.'

VPA

I was once told that to be really successful in business, especially in the service industry, you need Vision, Passion and Action. In 1899 the US Patent Office issued a statement to the effect that everything that could be invented already had been – they were reckoning without the VPA of people as yet unborn. Many people have one or two of these qualities but lack the third. Remember that VPA does not all have to come from one person, but can be achieved by putting the right people together, leadership and good team work.

> *'There are many things in life that will catch your eye, but only a few will catch your heart. Pursue those.'*

WILLPOWER

'If you think you are beaten ... you are.
If you think you dare not ... you don't.
If you'd like to win but you think you can't ...
it's almost a cinch you won't.
If you think you are losing ... you're lost. For out
in this world you will find:
Success begins with a fellow's will ... It's all
in the state of mind!'

'The difference between a successful person
and others is not a lack of strength, not a lack
of knowledge, but rather a lack of will.'

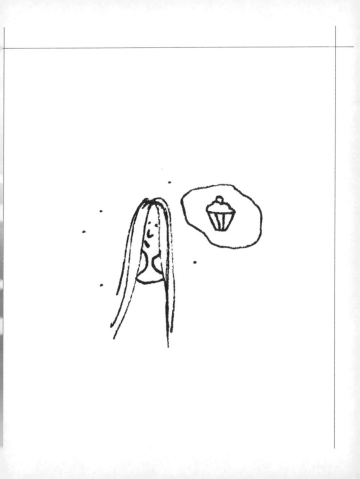

'Know ye what it is to be a child
It is to be something very different
from the person of today. It is to
have a spirit yet streaming from the
waters of baptism: it is to believe in
love, to believe in loveliness, to believe
in belief, it is to be so little that the
elves can reach to whisper in your ear,
it is to turn pumpkins into coaches and
mice into horses, lowness into loftiness,
and nothing into everything, for each child
has its fairy godmother in its own soul,
it is to live in a nutshell and count
yourself the king of infinite space.'

Francis Thompson

WONDERMENT

Spend time with children. Seeing the world through children's eyes can remind us how amazing, fascinating, interesting and wonderful so many things are that surround us, and that we have come to take for granted. Just look and you will see. Don't let cynicism take you over. Keep your innocence and wonderment, take a fresh look, be inquisitive and enjoy.

'Opportunities are disguised by hard work, so most people don't recognize them.'

'Find something you enjoy and you'll never work a day in your life.'

'To love what you do and feel that it matters –
how could anything be more fun?'

Katherine Graham

'The trouble with the rat race is that even if you win, you're still a rat.'

Lily Tomlin

'The race for quality has no finish line.'

'No one on their deathbed said: "I wish I'd spent more time at the office."'

WORK

Work is important. It feeds our self-respect and self-worth. It can give us purpose and a sense of achievement. It can stretch, develop and reward us. But make sure you have that all-important perspective: think about how your work impacts upon your loved ones. Don't miss out on life, fitness and good relationships. If you are unhappy with your job you are squandering your most precious possession: time. List all the things you enjoy and are good at, and everything positive about yourself. Then work out how to integrate these qualities into your daily routine – your job, your hobbies and your family life. And don't say you do not have the time.

'A violin cannot play a sweet note unless the strings are under pressure. Likewise we perform better under pressure. If you do put too much pressure on the strings they snap. So do we. When the violin is not being used, you release the tension on the strings. We too need periods of relaxation to recover and renew.'

WORK STRESS

It is very rare not to suffer from some kind of job-related stress. Deadlines, demanding bosses, intransigent team members, too much work, e-mail overload, long hours, budgets and sales target can all add up to an overwhelming burden, even if we love our work and respond to challenges. Certainly we need some sense of pressure to perform well, but too much is counter-productive. Try the strategies on p141 for easing work stress.

- ✿ Learn time-management techniques to improve organization and reduce clutter.
- ✿ Take time out to relax for at least 10 minutes every 2 hours, and take a healthy lunch break – preferably with a short walk outside.
- ✿ Obtain training in areas that will make you more effective.
- ✿ Don't procrastinate, prioritize.
- ✿ Understand how your work colleagues 'tick' and work with them, rather than against them.
- ✿ Have a life outside work and enjoy it – but be aware that excess consumption of alcohol and recreational drugs will reduce your work performance and make you feel sluggish and demotivated.
- ✿ Create a conscious barrier between work and home so that you leave the cares of the day behind when you return home.
- ✿ Counteract the mental activity of the day and burn off stress with some physical exercise.
- ✿ Identify what you enjoy about your job and constantly remind yourself of it!

WORRY

Worrigan is one of the oldest words in the dictionary. It comes from Anglo-Saxon times and means to 'throttle' or 'choke'. Worrying about something is one of the most pointless things you can do, particularly as most of the evils we imagine never happen. It twists you up inside, and the long-term health implications are similar to those caused by stress. To counteract these:

- ℗ Use the word 'concerned' instead of 'worried'.
- ℗ Take any practical steps you can take, then let whatever it is that is worrying you go and do something to take your mind off it.
- ℗ Or, defer your worrying to a certain time of day. Chances are, by the time you are ready to worry about it, you will have realized what a waste of energy it is.
- ℗ If you worry at night, keep a notepad by your bed, write down your thoughts and promise yourself you'll deal with them in the morning.

'Worry is like a rocking chair, it gives you something to do, but it doesn't get you anywhere.'

'You can't change the past, but you can ruin a perfectly good present by worrying about the future.'

'Beauty may be skin deep, but worry can seep to the very core of our being.'

Stephen Bowkett

'The line of the horizon does not exist except in our own minds.'

The Sanctuary in Covent Garden is a Day Spa and Fitness Club exclusively for women owned and operated by The Sanctuary Span Group, a company founded originally as Wheway Lifestyle International by Tanya and Allan Wheway in 1989. The Sanctuary Spa Group have recently opened Sanctuary Spas in David Lloyd Clubs located in Sidcup, Stevenage, Chigwell, Milton Keynes, Leeds and Manchester. A Sanctuary Spa and Fitness Club is located in the Lake District within Rank's Oasis Holiday Village and the latest to open is a Sanctuary Health Club and Spa within the new Kensington Hotel, London. All of these Sanctuary Spas welcome men as well as women.

The Sanctuary Spa Group provide worldwide consultancy in the spa business and created and commissioned the award-winning Chiva-Som health resort in Thailand. They are soon to open their first Sanctuary abroad on the Dead Sea in Jordan and have recently launched a range of Sanctuary Spa Products and their first CD.

THE SANCTUARY

Covent Garden, London

A DAY SPA EXCLUSIVELY
FOR WOMEN

Contact:

The Sanctuary
12 Floral Street
Covent Garden
London
WC2E 9DH

Telephone: 0171 420 5151
Fax: 0171 497 0410

for details of day and evening rates and treatments available.

Also available:

———————— ❧ ————————

TREASURES FROM THE SANCTUARY

FOR THE BODY

TREASURES FROM THE SANCTUARY

FOR THE SPIRIT

By Tanya Wheway

with Jane Ross-Macdonald

Words of inspiration and practical wisdom from The Sanctuary in Covent Garden, London.